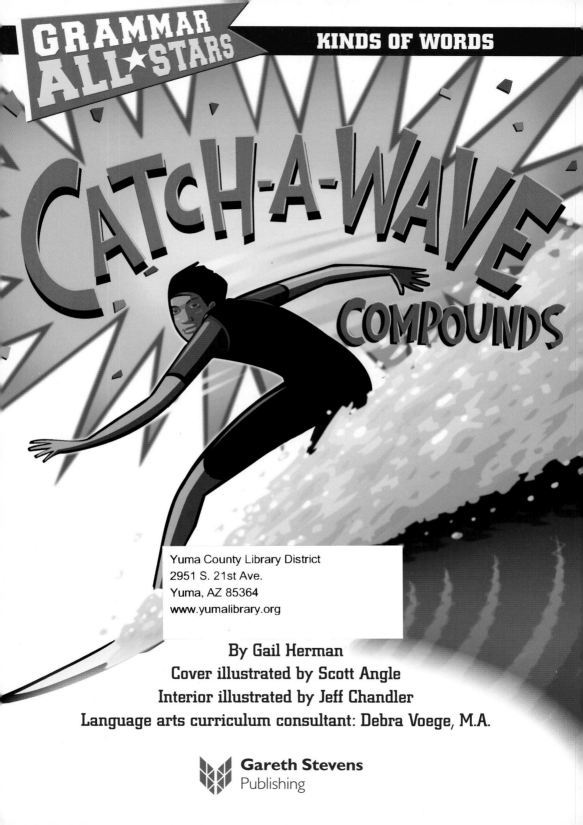

CATCH-A-WAVE
COMPOUNDS

By Gail Herman
Cover illustrated by Scott Angle
Interior illustrated by Jeff Chandler
Language arts curriculum consultant: Debra Voege, M.A.

Gareth Stevens
Publishing

Please visit our web site at **www.garethstevens.com**.
For a free color catalog describing Gareth Stevens Publishing's list of
high-quality books, call 1-800-542-2595 (USA) or 1-800-387-3178 (Canada).
Gareth Stevens Publishing's fax: 1-877-542-2596

Library of Congress Cataloging-in-Publication Data

Herman, Gail, 1959–
      Catch-a-wave compounds / by Gail Herman; illustrated by Jeff
Chandler; language arts curriculum consultant: Debra Voege, M.A.
         p. cm. — (Grammar all-stars: kinds of words)
      At head of title: Grammar all-stars: kinds of words
      Includes bibliographical references and index.
      ISBN-10: 1-4339-0008-4   ISBN-13: 978-1-4339-0008-2 (lib. bdg.)
      ISBN-10: 1-4339-0149-8   ISBN-13: 978-1-4339-0149-2 (pbk.)
      1. English language—Compound words—Juvenile literature. 2. English language—
Word formation—Juvenile literature. 3. English language—Grammar—Juvenile literature.
I. Voege, Debra. II. Title. III. Title: Grammar all-stars: kinds of words.
    PE1175.H47   2008
    428.1'3—dc22   2008030387

This edition first published in 2009 by
Gareth Stevens Publishing
A Weekly Reader® Company
1 Reader's Digest Road
Pleasantville, NY 10570-7000 USA

Copyright © 2009 by Gareth Stevens, Inc.

Executive Managing Editor: Lisa M. Herrington
Senior Editor: Barbara Bakowski
Creative Director: Lisa Donovan
Art Director: Ken Crossland
Publisher: Keith Garton

Printed in the United States of America

1 2 3 4 5 6 7 8 9 10 09 08

May 2009

CONTENTS

Look for the **boldface** words on each page.
Then read the **HANG-TEN HINT** that follows.

CHAPTER 1

SURF'S UP!

What Are Closed Compounds?

"Sun, surf, and sports—my three favorite things!" says P-L-A-Y TV announcer Buzz Star. He pulls his car off the **highway**. "Time to hit the beach!" he says. Buzz looks toward the **shoreline**. "Now, where can Dylan Jacob Foote be? He's my kid reporter today."

"Buzz! Dude! I'm over here! I'm setting up drinks for the surfers!"

Buzz looks at the sign on the **boardwalk**. It reads: D.J.'s Lemon Ade.

"Hmm," Buzz says. "I see that you like to be called D.J." D.J. nods. "I also see that you're confused about closed compound words."

"What is a closed compound word?" D.J. asks.

"A closed compound word is made by putting together two or more smaller words, like *lemon* and *ade*."

HANG-TEN HINT

CLOSED COMPOUNDS

A **closed compound** is made up of two or more smaller words joined to make a new word.

D.J. frowns. "You mean it should be **lemonade**?"

"That's right! But it's an easy fix." Buzz folds the sign so that there is no space between the words. "**Sometimes** compound words are tricky, D.J." Buzz looks at his **wristwatch**. "It's almost time for us to go on the air! If you point out cool stuff about the competition, I'll point out compound words along the way."

"Sure," says D.J. "But first I have to put on **sunblock**. I don't want to get a **sunburn**."

"You've aleady named two compound words!" exclaims Buzz. He slips on his **sunglasses**.

The camera operator holds up three fingers. "Buzz, we're live in three ... two ... one ..."

HANG-TEN HINT

CLOSED COMPOUNDS

Are you ever unsure whether two words should be written separately or combined as one? The best place to go for the answer: **a dictionary**!

LIVE

PLAYTV **THE COWABUNGA CLASSIC**

Buzz looks into the camera. "Aloha, surfing fans! This **weekend** I'm at Big Break Beach. Surfers from around the world are gathering here. The Cowabunga Classic is the biggest surfing contest of the season! Kid reporter D.J. Foote is helping me. His mom, Sandy Foote, is one of the surfers in today's event. D.J. knows surfing, so he'll show us around."

D.J. leads Buzz to a row of **surfboards**. "The surfers keep their boards here."

"Hi, D.J.!" **somebody** shouts. A **lifeguard** sees the TV crew. She waves from her chair. "I'll be cheering for your mom!"

"Thanks, Sunny!" D.J. replies. Then he points to a group of surfers wearing **wetsuits**. "My mom is over there. Hi, Mom!" he calls.

Sandy Foote is waxing her board. D.J. takes Buzz to meet his mother. After a **handshake**, Sandy points at the ocean. "Look at those **whitecaps**! I can't wait to surf!"

Whoosh! A giant wave hits the **seashore** just as Buzz takes out his reporter's **notebook**. He groans. "Yikes! Too bad it isn't **waterproof**!"

"Hold on tight, Buzz," D.J. cries. "Here comes **Wipeout** Williams!"

"*Wipeout* is another compound word," Buzz says.

Crash! A surfer barrels **headfirst** into Buzz, who falls to the sand.

"That's Wipeout!" says D.J. "He's a real **daredevil**."

Wipeout tumbles into the water at the ocean's edge. When he stands up, his head is covered with **seaweed**. "Sorry about that, dude!"

Buzz brushes sand from his shirt. "I hope his balance is better on a **surfboard**!"

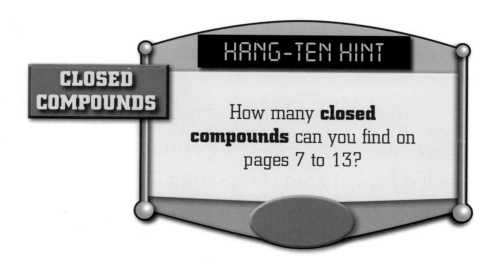

CLOSED COMPOUNDS

HANG-TEN HINT

How many **closed compounds** can you find on pages 7 to 13?

CHAPTER 2

HIGH-FIVE SURFING

What Are Hyphenated Compounds?

"Here we go, surfing fans," Buzz announces. "The contest is about to start. D.J., tell our viewers what is happening."

"The surfers have left the **check-in** table," D.J. comments. "Now they're stretching at the **warm-up** area."

"You just used two compound words," Buzz says. "*Check-in* and *warm-up* are called hyphenated compounds."

"Awesome!" D.J. gives Buzz a **high-five**.

HANG-TEN HINT

HYPHENATED COMPOUNDS

Hyphenated compounds are two or more words linked by hyphens. Hyphens are often used when words would be confusing without them.

Buzz explains how the Cowabunga Classic works. "There are three heats, or contests. The winners of each heat compete in the final round. Look, the surfers in the first heat are paddling out! There goes your mom, D.J."

"She's a real pro," D.J. says. "Mom got her first board when she was a kid. My **great-grandfather** gave it to her."

"Now each surfer will try to catch the perfect wave," Buzz explains.

"Mom's really hanging ten," D.J. says. "Ten toes on the nose—of the surfboard, of course. She's getting max speed, making a bottom turn. Now she's climbing the face of the wave! Boosting some air there. Totally excellent!"

"The judges give Sandy Foote a score of 9.6!" Buzz reports.

"Here's Wipeout Williams, paddling out late," adds D.J. "Uh-oh! The tide is turning him around. He's doing an **about-face**!" D.J. shakes his head. "Wipeout bails."

Buzz takes over. "Wipeout pops out of the surf like a **jack-in-the-box**. Now he's washing up on the shore."

"Watch out, Wipeout!" D.J. shouts. The surfer is headed straight for a big sandcastle. D.J. groans. "Wipeout's score: zero!"

Wipeout stumbles from the water and shakes sand from his hair. "Dude," he says to D.J. "That was a totally rad ride!"

Buzz shrugs his shoulders. "Wipeout is a **happy-go-lucky** guy." He turns back toward the waves. "The other surfers have some good moves. Mary Lou Malibu makes a good bottom turn with a lot of speed. Then she cuts up the face of the wave."

"She hit the lip of the wave and got major air!" D.J. says. "Now Deck Dunzo does a sweet **one-eighty**. He can really carve it up!"

"I'll do the **wrap-up**, D.J.," says Buzz. "The judges are tallying the surfers' scores. The winner of the first heat is … " D.J. crosses his fingers. "It's Sandy Foote!" Buzz shouts. "She will go on to the final round!"

D.J. runs to his mom and hangs a chain of **forget-me-not** flowers around her neck. "You rock, Mom!"

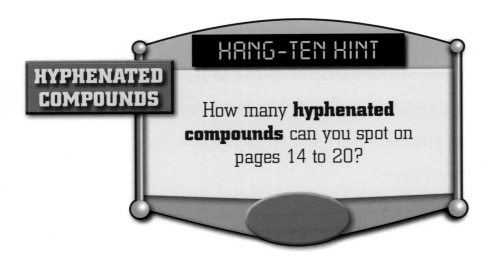

HANG-TEN HINT

HYPHENATED COMPOUNDS

How many **hyphenated compounds** can you spot on pages 14 to 20?

CHAPTER 3

COWABUNGA, DUDE!
What Are Open Compounds?

"It's the final round of the Cowabunga Classic," Buzz tells the TV audience. "Sandy Foote, Rad Dewd, and Charlie Narly are hoping to find some monster waves. D.J., tell us about Rad and Charlie while the surfers paddle out."

"Well, Rad is still in **high school**. He has already won a lot of surfing trophies. Then there's Charlie. He's in great shape. He likes to eat **peanut butter** for energy. He also eats a lot of **health food**. He even feeds natural treats to his **house cat**."

HANG-TEN HINT

OPEN COMPOUNDS

An **open compound** is a combination of words that represents a single idea. The words are always in specific order. Changing the order would change the meaning.

23

Buzz looks toward the ocean. "The surfers are dropping in," he says. "What a **takeoff**! Charlie does a **three-sixty**."

"Rad goes into a high aerial," adds D.J. "He flies off the crest of the wave and hangs in the air. He's still **airborne**! Finally Rad drops back on the face of the wave. He stays **upright**. Whoa, that was classic!"

"Here's your mom, riding the tube," Buzz continues. "That's a tough move, but will she pull off a win?"

D.J. sighs. "I guess not. The judges give Rad a perfect 10! Mom and Charlie each score a 9."

"Be on the **lookout**," Buzz warns.
"Here comes **Wipeout** Williams."

Wipeout catches his **flip-flop** on the
nose of a **surfboard**. The board flips in
the air … and lands safely on a **beach
ball**! Wipeout flashes Buzz a **thumbs-up**.
"No worries, dude."

Buzz faces the camera. "Thanks for
joining us at the Cowabunga Classic.
I hope you had a ball at the beach!"
He turns to D.J. "Let's surf on over to
the Snack Shack for some **hot dogs**
and **popcorn**!"

When the surfers reach the shore, D.J. hugs his mother. "Sorry you didn't win the trophy, Mom."

"I have **something** better than a trophy," Sandy tells D.J. She holds up the **necklace** of **forget-me-nots**.

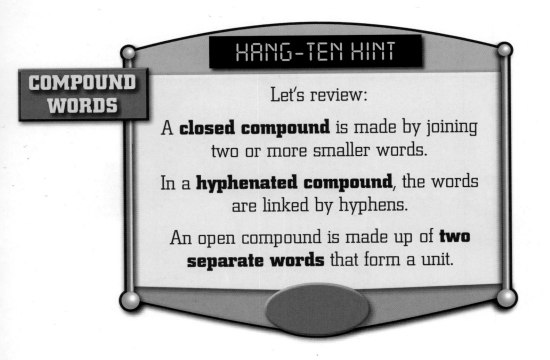

HANG-TEN HINT

COMPOUND WORDS

Let's review:

A **closed compound** is made by joining two or more smaller words.

In a **hyphenated compound**, the words are linked by hyphens.

An open compound is made up of **two separate words** that form a unit.

BUZZ STAR PLAYS BY THE RULES!

A **closed compound** is made up of two or more smaller words joined to make a new word.
Examples: shore + line = shoreline   lemon + ade = lemonade
         pop + corn = popcorn   surf + board = surfboard

In a **hyphenated compound**, two or more words are linked by hyphens. Hyphens are often used when words would be confusing without them.
Examples: check-in, warm-up, high-five, flip-flop

An **open compound** is a combination of words that represents a single idea. The words are always in specific order. Changing the order would change the meaning.
Examples: high school, house cat, peanut butter, beach ball

Are you unsure whether two words should be written separately, hyphenated, or combined as one word? Check a **dictionary**!

ALL-STAR ACTIVITY

D.J. wrote an article for *Totally Tubular Surf* magazine.
On a piece of paper, **list all the closed compounds**.

Surf Showdown   By D.J. Foote

What is it like to have a surfer as your mom? It's the coolest! My mom, Sandy Foote, totally rocked at the Cowabunga Classic. Surfing's superstars met at Big Break Beach for the contest. Fans crowded the boardwalk and shoreline to watch the action. Some beachcombers collected sand dollars and seashells.

The final round was a face-off between the top three surfers. What a nail-biter! My mom finished second only to the big winner, Rad Dewd. His surfboard moves were crazy! After Rad picked up his trophy, an airplane flew by. It left a message in skywriting: Congratulations, Surfers!

Suddenly, the sky clouded over. I thought we were in for a really big downpour. But the clouds were gone by sunset, just in time for the fireworks!

The next day, the locals took us to one of their favorite hangouts. It was a fair, with a Ferris wheel and a merry-go-round. There was plenty of food, too, like cotton candy and popcorn. I had a lifetime of fun in just one weekend!

All-Star Challenge

List all the **hyphenated compounds** and **open compounds** in D.J.'s article.

Turn the page to check your answers and to see how many points you scored!

31

Did you find enough closed compounds to win the Cowabunga Classic?

1–4 closed compounds: Wipeout!   **9–12** closed compounds: Big Air!

5–8 closed compounds: You Bailed!   **13–16** closed compounds: COWABUNGA!

CLOSED COMPOUNDS

1. Showdown
2. superstars
3. boardwalk
4. shoreline
5. beachcombers
6. seashells
7. surfboard
8. airplane
9. skywriting
10. downpour
11. sunset
12. fireworks
13. hangouts
14. popcorn
15. lifetime
16. weekend

All-Star Challenge

Hyphenated Compounds
1. face-off
2. nail-biter
3. merry-go-round

Open Compounds
1. sand dollars
2. Ferris wheel
3. cotton candy